I'm Still Standing

Jeanette Bradley

To my Heavenly Father, thank You for redeeming my life. Thank You for Your love, mercy, and grace. You brought me out of hell and gave me heaven on earth. You've saved me, healed me, delivered me, and redeemed me. My life wasn't worth living until I gave it all to You. I will follow You all my days.

To every hurting and lost soul out there, for anyone who's tired of running on empty . . . this is for you. And this is to glorify our wonderful God.

Acknowledgements

Thank you to Brandon and Chuckie, both great sons and even better husbands and fathers. And to my loving daughters-in-law Amanda and Alejandra, thank you for your beautiful hearts and for loving my sons and granddaughters the way you do. Thank you to my awesome granddaughters, Haley and Maddy Mae; you give my life such meaning.

Thank you to my wonderful cousin, Donna. You've always been there for me. You've made time to listen and helped put the pieces of my heart back together again. Thank you Mom for all you've done for me. Life hasn't always been easy, but I know God is blessing us more and more every day. I'm thankful you're my Mom, I love you. Terrie, I'm so grateful you're my sister. Thank you for helping me when I needed it. To my wonderful nephew and nieces, Stawn, Grace, and Heather, thank you for always showing me love and kindness. Your mother would be proud. Thank you Lilly for your great patience with my picture for the book.

Thank you to Pastor Rice, Pastor Duble, and my spiritual mothers Carol, Eileen, and Kathy. I thank you Pam for being such a great and prayerful editor. I can't leave out Joyce, thank you for all your gracious guidance and advice. You're awesome, too. I love you all, and I pray God's best for every one of you.

Table of Contents

Introduction

Innocence is a priceless gift from God. Ideally, you live out your childhood with few cares except maybe what you'll do the next day or how you'll talk your parents into buying you a new toy. I believe we take happy memories for granted. Never forget how blessed you are if you've had a happy childhood and have fond teenage memories.

For me, the trauma of abuse caused a lifetime of misery and suffering. I felt so trapped that I wasn't able to move forward and live well. I settled for whatever came my way, because I felt so worthless. Don't let this happen to you. Speak up. Stand up. Let your pain be your power. God made my mess my message, and He can do the same for you.

If you take away anything from my story, I hope you'll see the importance of reaching out for help. Don't let fear, or shame, or anything or anyone keep you from getting help and healing. We don't have to let life, our circumstances, or others define us. Failing is not falling down, it's staying down.

I believe my sister Debbie died at least twenty years before her time because of the devastation of lifelong trauma. Unresolved trauma takes a high toll on our health, not just physically, but emotionally and spiritually. Debbie never knew the freedom and true peace that should have been hers.

On the other hand, I'm determined to do my best every day and try to offer hope to others any way I can. I want anyone who has suffered any type of abuse or injustice to see that there is life after trauma. To be part of the problem or part of the solution is a daily decision. I choose to be part of the solution. That's why I wrote this book.

We don't have to be lifelong victims. We can have victory, freedom, peace, and joy. My "rescue" began when I gave my heart to God. He picked up the pieces of my shattered life and has lovingly continued to put them back together. I finally feel whole and free.

I pray that after you read my story, you too will begin your journey of hope and freedom. Let it start today.

Chapter 1

Innocence Lost

"Innocence is always unsuspicious."
Thomas C. Haliburton

My family roots go back to the hills of Kentucky. My father, his father, and his grandfather before him were all coal miners. Not only were the men in my father's family strong, but the women, too. "Back up in the holler," they didn't have the luxury of modern conveniences. They toted buckets of water from the well and worked the garden day and night. While the men worked the mine, the women canned, did housework, and made clothes and quilts. It was a hard but good life.

Very much in love, my parents married young, when Mom was fifteen and Dad was twenty or so. In fact, Dad was most likely Mom's first love. My sister Debbie was born within a year, followed in fifteen months by my sister Carrie. Mom became pregnant with me soon after.

When Dad was twenty-six, he got rheumatic fever. He was slowly recovering and should have stayed off work longer. One routine morning, Mom woke up and told Dad she'd make breakfast. Dad said, "Okay." She heard him raise the window, and that was it. Dad suffered a heart attack. He never recovered, and died a short time later. She learned later that it was his heart.

Heartbroken, in shock, and eight months pregnant with me, Mom took her two babies and moved to Mansfield, Ohio, to live with her brother and his wife and to be closer to Dad in the hospital. Because of her grief, she almost lost me and had to put me on a pillow next to her in bed, she was in such deep grief, she found it hard to even hold me.

Imagine being a widow at eighteen with three children. The sorrow must have been unbearable. But Mom was strong. She used Dad's insurance money to buy Grandma and Grandpa a farm in southern Ohio. Most of our happy memories are from life on that farm.

There was the Omar Bread man, who'd come once a month. We'd climb into his truck to smell all the sweet rolls and cakes. We'd sometimes play in the orchard down the road, where once, we narrowly escaped a bull that chased us up a tree. Grandma would take us berry picking whenever she wanted to make blackberry dumplings. They were the best you ever tasted!

Things started to change by the time I reached junior high school.

Have you ever felt terror, real in-the-gut, bone-chilling terror? The kind that makes you tense up and hurt all over? That kind of life-changing terror began for my sister Debbie and me when I was twelve.

Until then, life had been pretty good. I enjoyed the usual childhood things, like playing Barbie for hours with my cousin Donna or some other memorable game like hide 'n seek. On one family vacation, we explored Mammoth Caves in Kentucky. On another, we visited New England. One year, my stepdad offered us each fifty dollars to stay home with the promise that he'd cook all our meals, whatever we wanted. Vacation with six females (and a female dog) was a little more than he could take.

But, in the blink of an eye, our lives changed.

When a traumatic event interrupts normal growth, it's called "arrested development." Learning stops and you stay "stuck" at a particular age until you get help or something changes. The effects can be devastating.

When I was twelve and Debbie just fourteen, we saw an opportunity to get out of school for a few days, and invited ourselves on our stepfather's out-of-town trip. We thought it would be fun and headed to New York with wide-eyed excitement.

I remember the first night we stayed in a small, cheap motel room. Our stepfather had bought a six-pack of beer. Debbie and I were sorting through our suitcases when he offered us some. Confused and afraid, I took one beer for both of us and led Debbie to the privacy of the bathroom to change into our pajamas. Still, chills were creeping up the back of my spine. What was going on? What was he doing? What should we do?

We changed quickly, and I suggested we both take a sip of beer and pour out the rest. That way, he'd smell it on us and remain calm. Overwhelmed with the sense to protect us, I would later believe that what was about to happen was my fault. (I carried "survivor's guilt" until I was fifty-nine years old.)

Debbie and I huddled close together in one bed, when he rose from the other and reached for my arm. But Debbie reached across me and said, "No, take me." Scared and disoriented, I just lay there, trembling. He covered my head so I couldn't see, but I heard strange sounds and peeked out from the covers. With him on top of her, Debbie lay there lifeless and crying—suffering in silence. But that didn't stop him.

When it was finally over, she crawled back into bed with me, shaking violently. I held her close and remember trying to comfort her. I suggested that we sneak out to the rental office and call the police once he fell asleep, but Debbie said no. Looking back, I believe she was afraid that if we'd tried and failed, he would come after me next, or worse. All she could do was tremble in fear. So we lay there holding each other and kept watch until daybreak.

By the grace of God, I have absolutely no memory of the rest of the trip, not a single detail. But I don't know how we could have acted normal after that.

If you've been molested or suffered sexual abuse, don't believe the lie that you brought it on yourself or that you must have done something to deserve it. Someone *will* believe you. Let your voice be heard, and don't stop until someone listens. Your pain matters. You matter.

By staying silent, the fear gets greater and the shame goes deeper. Your soul takes in those lies, and it changes you. You can't love yourself *and* take the blame for everything that goes wrong in your life. You'll justify more abuse, trauma, and the pain that goes down to your bones because you're so used to the darkness in your soul. You'll accept whatever circumstance you're in, no matter how wrong.

Life is too short. Don't let the lies win.

It's hard to predict the long-term effects of trauma. Sometimes darkness becomes our *normal*. The damage can last a lifetime. I know from experience. I remained an addict and alcoholic for almost thirty years to avoid the pain that was there every morning. But there *is* hope. I found mine in Jesus. He's been my redeeming grace. He brought me out of my personal hell.

Sadly, Debbie internalized everything. If she talked at all about her trauma, it was usually only with me. I still struggle with the feeling that I let her down, that I should've done something—protected or rescued her.

Most of my pain and trauma were externalized. I lived and loved hard, no matter what the cost. When a man proposed to me, I thought I had to marry him or I'd lose him, so I ended up with five husbands and six marriages. Unable to cope with emptiness or loss, I had no limits. Numb from emotional pain, you couldn't hurt me. If you did me wrong, I'd do you wrong. The walls I'd built to keep others out also kept out joy and deprived me of a happy, loving, peaceful life.

Self-preservation is a strong motive to do desperate things. My spirit was like a bulldozer. I'd take down whoever got in my way and whatever threatened what little heart I had left. I'd hurt you before you could hurt me. I'd forgotten how to love and be loved. If you can't receive love, you can't believe love. If you feel unworthy, you act unworthy.

Unhealed pain and suffering cause a vicious cyclone of madness that can't be stopped on your own. I tried to calm the storm with drugs, alcohol, and men. I'd drink every day until I blacked out. I'd lose track of my car and wake up with strange men. I'd smoke crack until I was so weak that I had to rely on other junkies to light the crack stem for me. I tried whatever would ease the pain. The cost didn't matter; there was no price too high. That's insanity!

I never once stopped to think about my future. I wouldn't let myself dream, because I couldn't face unattainable goals. I was too damaged to believe anything good would ever happen for me or come from me. But that was before Debbie led me to the Lord and mentored me in the faith. She became a powerful woman of God and touched hundreds of lives. A wonderful sister, mother, aunt, and Grammy, she was a great blessing to me and was my close friend. We had a bond that could not be broken.

I remember sitting for hours and talking about our dreams for the future. We'd always wanted a huge barn for the homeless, the poor, and the outcasts—a place where they'd learn to feel good about themselves and start their lives over. We wanted them to know that somebody cared—that they were worth being loved.

Debbie passed away from cervical cancer on April 1, 2012. It was a long and painful journey, but she fought the good fight of faith. I believe all abuse survivors deserve to die with dignity. More importantly, I believe they deserve to live with dignity.

I can't help but grieve her life more than her death, and what could have been, what should have been. I miss her dearly, but know that she's no longer in pain. I hope to carry on and bring our dream to pass.

It may have been the deep fear, shame, anger, and resentment she carried all her life that caused Debbie to neglect her health. I think she may have been too self-conscious or ashamed to get regular check-ups, so the cancer was caught too late. Please consider this a wake-up call. Don't shut out love and life and let those who have harmed you win. Speak up. Reach out. Don't wait.

Debbie eventually forgave our stepfather, who passed away on August 27, 2012. Her three amazing children and four wonderful grandchildren are all "cut from the same cloth" as Debbie. I'm so thankful to be a part of their lives and see what wonderful and loving human beings they are. I know she would be so proud of them!

She left a beautiful legacy of love, perseverance, faith, and forgiveness. I know Debbie's descendants will continue to make a difference in the lives of many. My life has been touched profoundly and is so much richer because of them.

Chapter 2

Wild Child

"I wish I was the white crayon.
Then no one would use me."
Author Unknown

If you've ever gotten lost while driving, you know it can be pretty scary, especially when night falls and you're in a strange place. You don't feel safe. You want to ask for directions, but you're afraid to get out of the car. You don't know anyone, so you don't ask for help.

That's the way it felt after the sexual abuse began. It was always tormenting; I never knew what was going to happen. I was continuously hyper-vigilant. Without much rest, I was always on the defensive. This went on for two years.

I'll never forget the day I heard my name being called over the public address system at school. I was told to report to the principal's office immediately; it was urgent. I'm not sure why, but down in my gut, I knew what had happened.

I was escorted into the room, where Mom and Debbie sat. A police woman stood behind them against the wall. At her breaking point, Debbie had finally reported the incest. After hearing my side of the story, the principal asked Mom what she thought. Amazingly, Mom didn't believe us. To her, we just *couldn't* be telling the truth. I felt like I'd been punched in the stomach. Who'd make up something like that? I was in a living nightmare and couldn't wake up. Debbie and I were in shock.

I don't remember exactly what happened next, but the police must have pursued the case. Our stepfather had to move into a motel while the court hearing went on. Mom would take all three of us in a cab to the motel to visit. But Debbie and I refused to see him, so we'd wait while she and Carrie went in.

I never gave these details much thought until my search for understanding led me to realize that we all handle devastation differently. What could make a mother choose a man over her own children? How could sexually abused children be expected to visit the stepfather who had traumatized them? Mom may have been as shocked and frightened as we were. Her whole world had been turned upside down. How could the man she loved and admired do something so evil to her daughters? What could she do now? How would she survive? Not knowing where to go for help, she stood by his side, no matter the cost.

Months passed, and life settled into a routine. It was the late 1960s, and like other kids back then, we would hang out with friends, play records, and dance a night or two a week. When Dad would sometimes have to drive our girlfriends home, it was always nerve wracking. I'd be on guard to protect them from what might happen. I felt responsible for keeping them safe.

Then I'd have to fight him off on the ride home.

One time, he pulled off on the side of the road and tried to rape me. He finally stopped when I fought back. I went straight to bed and propped the usual chair under our bedroom doorknob to feel safe. Now, added to the trauma of Debbie being raped, was my own victimization.

During those two long years, the joy of being a happy-go-lucky teenager was drained from my life. Gone were the days to hang out with friends, laugh at silly things, make daily discoveries, and simply enjoy being alive. The incest and sexual abuse had robbed me of it all.

Instead, there was shame, fear, distrust, and sorrow. I wasn't just ashamed, I became shame. (It can define you, if you let it.) I was too young to fight it and didn't have a clue how to handle it. With no support system and no one to trust, my world became smaller and smaller. So, I took the low road and started smoking at twelve, drinking at thirteen, and soon discovered boys. You know that old song, "Lookin' for Love in All the Wrong Places"? Well, that's how it all started.

My self-esteem was just about on empty, but I headed off, full steam ahead. I had no limits, but even worse, no normal, no sense of self, no need to be cautious or think ahead about consequences. It didn't matter, because I didn't matter. I couldn't live up to what others wanted me to be. With every mistake, I felt increasingly useless.

Without direction, guidance, or stability, my family was torn apart. Debbie went to live with Grandma, and Carrie and I stayed with Mom and Dad. Nothing was ever the same after that.

In the ninth grade, I remember running away just because I wanted to do something different. It was crazy. I can't recall if my girlfriend Sue or I came up with the brilliant idea, but we took off right before the homeroom bell.

Sue was something else. She thought she was a witch. She was always playing with a Ouija board. She'd take me into the school bathroom, turn off the lights, and cast spells. She was my friend, but I was scared of her—especially when she did things like show me a piece of paper with one word in the middle—*death.*

The day we made our escape, we pooled our money (less than four dollars), thumbed out to my Grandma's, asked her for a few more dollars, and took off again. We were goofy enough to switch clothes behind a shack in a field, so that if we were caught, our clothes wouldn't match the authority's description.

After panhandling all day, we ended up in a little town about an hour and a half from home. We had planned to buy a bottle of aspirin and kill ourselves, but we chickened out. Later that night, we turned ourselves in. We were accused of stealing a car from Columbus, until it was realized that we didn't even know how to drive.

Mom and Dad came to get me, and I was grounded for a while but didn't get into serious trouble like I thought I would. That was strange, but I was glad. Debbie ran away a short time later, but what happened to her was awful.

Our stepdad started to beat her in the kitchen and pushed her all the way up to her bedroom. It seemed like an eternity listening to the crack of that belt and her helpless screams. I don't know why I didn't run to help her. I guess I was too scared.

I felt guilty every time she was whipped or got into trouble. I would give anything to have rescued her from all the abuse she continued to endure at his hands. I believe this was when the seed of addiction was planted in me. Dad would never beat me, but he sure loved to beat Debbie. I would suffer sexual abuse for some time to come, but it was nothing compared to what she went through.

The summer that changed my life and helped ease my pain was the summer I met a cute blue-eyed, blond-haired boy named Joe. My sisters and I spent most of our junior-high summers with Grandma. She lived in a small town across from a ballpark. During a baseball game with friends, I was pitching and noticed Joe watching at the top of the hill. I knew it had to be love at first sight, because I'd never felt so good inside.

We'd talk about living in the Teton mountains and even named the kids we'd have. We went to the county fair. We wrote love letters to each other. I couldn't wait to hear his soft, sweet voice on the phone. I felt safe in his arms, the load I carried seemed lighter, and life started making sense again.

One night we'd hung out all evening at Grandma's and watched a movie. When I found out he had to go to work, I was upset. He worked at his brother's restaurant, and I was jealous of a pretty, blond waitress who worked there. When I couldn't convince him to stay, my wounded, 15-year-old mind ran wild with thoughts of them working together all night, so I decided to take a walk to sort things out.

I believed we were soul mates; nothing would ever change that. He'd even given me his ring. I was head-over-heels in love and thought the feelings were mutual. I knew he'd be coming home later, and we'd be together again tomorrow. It seemed enough.

Chapter 3

The End of Me, the Beginning of Shame

"Loneliness and the feeling of being unwanted is the most terrible poverty."
Mother Theresa

I was still pretty upset when I got up the next day, since Joe had gone to work despite my pleadings. I decided to take a walk "uptown" to see what was happening and to buy some smokes. When I was leaving the store, a guy pulled up on a motorcycle. We glanced at each other, and I noticed he was cute. As I was walking away, he struck up a conversation and eventually invited me to go for a ride on his bike.

It was a beautiful summer afternoon and I thought, "What's the harm in a little bike ride in the country?" I was feeling rejected and thought the ride might help. Besides, this might make Joe jealous. I was so naïve, clueless to what was about to happen.

Thinking I'd only be gone for a short ride, I didn't bother to tell Grandma or anyone else where I was going or who I was with. We rode for a while out in the countryside, and then took some dirt roads. We met up with a guy in a car, and I ended up sitting between them in the front seat. I remember them giving me whisky before I got dizzy and blacked out.

Later, I was told to crawl through a window into a "clubhouse" next to the woods behind an old home. I remember nude pin-ups covering the walls and a set of bunk beds and a few chairs. There was a young girl sitting on the edge of the bed; she looked as scared as I felt, so I sat down next to her.

My next memory was waking up in a hospital hallway on a gurney in a straightjacket. I overheard the doctors telling my family that I'd been found in a ditch and brought to the emergency room. I had drugs and alcohol in my system and had been raped multiple times.

I'm not sure how long I was there, but I was finally released to my family in the hospital waiting area, where a relative brashly called me a whore. I couldn't believe it, after what I'd just gone through. How could anyone—especially a family member—label me anything but a victim, when I had been kidnapped and gang-raped? I was totally devastated.

The next day, a mutual friend of Joe's visited. He'd been the one who'd rescued me from ditch and told me what had happened, who'd done it, and how he'd found me. I was home alone and remember him following me into the kitchen. There was blood dripping from my hands onto the floor. I'd slit both my wrists. He rushed me to the sink and did the best he could to patch me up. This would be the first of many failed suicide attempts. Thank God for His mercy.

The doctors said I was manically depressed. I couldn't talk, eat, or even dress myself. I just sat there catatonic and silently waged war with the demons inside me. A few days later, I was scheduled to go to the hospital to have a clinical abortion, because I hadn't started my period. That's how rape cases were handled in the 1960s.

By mid-morning, Mom had dressed me and was brushing my hair. With every harsh jerk of the brush, she wondered what the neighbors would think and how I could have done such a thing. It was in the newspaper, after all. I wanted to cry out, but could only sit at the edge of the bed, beaten down by her torturous remarks.

I felt as if I were being slowly driven insane and was helpless to do anything about it. The sorrow and despair were so overwhelming that I can still remember how it cut me to the bone and ripped out the rest of my heart. When she finished, I went to the bathroom and discovered that I'd started my period. I was so thankful I didn't have to suffer through an abortion. I praise God so much for that now.

Joe and I broke up after that. He was a preacher's son. Maybe the publicity from the newspapers was too much for his family to bear. Maybe he was ashamed of me. I don't know.

I didn't think my heart could break any more, but I went numb inside. This terrible ordeal had ruined me. Who was I now? It didn't matter anymore, I didn't matter anymore, or at least that's how I felt. The trauma of needing a mother's love and not getting it was worse than the rape itself.

I barely went to school and did as little homework as possible to get by. Who cared? I'd go down to the OSU campus on Pearl Alley, hang out at different apartments, get high, meet guys, and fall in love for a day. Once I met a policewoman who turned out to be a very good friend. I'd cut school and go down to the police station just to sit and talk with her. She was willing to listen, and I felt like someone cared enough to let me talk. I needed to feel wanted.

I'd given up expecting love from my family, so I became promiscuous. Nothing hard core, just falling in love every other month and giving my heart and body away. I'd let others control me, especially men, for fear I'd lose or anger them. For me, sex equaled love. Six months into my senior year, I met my first husband, a Viet Nam veteran six years my senior.

Chapter 4

The Price I Paid for "Love"

"The soul would have no rainbow
had the eyes no tears."
John Vance Chaney

I was convinced I'd found true love this time. My husband, "Darren," was handsome, charming, a good provider, ambitious, and seemed attentive. But what did I know? I was a kid, just seventeen when we married. I wanted out of my house, and this was the answer. It didn't matter that I hadn't taken the time to get to know Darren. I believed everything he said to me.

We had a small wedding, but no honeymoon, and settled into a small apartment. Trying to create happy memories and show him how special he was to me, I dressed up every month on our anniversary date and fixed a nice candlelit dinner, holding onto the hope that I could have a happy life.

When a couple of girlfriends from high school came over for our one-year anniversary, I found out through the course of the evening that Darren had dated one of them during the entire first year of our marriage. This was the beginning of many infidelities. He ran around with women throughout our marriage and was abusive in almost every way. Although heartbroken, I stayed.

I excused his behavior, believing he too was broken and had no love to give. But his cold, affectionless treatment, lack of encouragement, and verbal abuse were so very hard on me. It got to the point that, for my own peace of mind, I'd pack his bags so he could head out for the weekend to be with his women.

Eventually, I escaped by drowning my sorrows. Thus began my new pattern of coping. I'd drink myself into oblivion to dull the pain, and when that didn't work, I'd slit my wrists. After one failed attempt, Darren offered to help me the next time I tried. It didn't end there. I took a whole bottle of aspirin once and even tried to hang myself, but the bar broke in the closet.

After almost six years of enduring the marriage, a wonderful, unplanned thing happened. I became pregnant. I remember sharing the news on Valentine's Day with Debbie and Mom and then Darren's mother. She was a sweet little lady and, like me, was happy and excited about her first grandchild. Sadly, the next morning we got a call that Darren's mother had died in her sleep. Still, I was thankful that she went to heaven knowing about the baby.

On October 5, 1976, my beautiful son, Brandon, was born. He was perfect in every way. For the first year, I took him to a department store every month to have pictures made. Mom and Debbie never seemed to tire of my endless questions about the do's and don'ts of babies. But Darren never wanted children and wouldn't let me hold Brandon when he'd cry. Here was my beautiful baby boy crying out for me, and I was not allowed to pick him up and comfort him. Every time he'd cry, I'd cry inside. But I was too afraid of Darren's temper to disobey.

During the blizzard of 1976, when Brandon was two months old, Darren moved out with his new girlfriend, leaving us without diapers or formula and with very little food. I had no idea how to handle a baby and look for work and feared for our future. Even so, Brandon was the best thing that ever happened to me. He gave me hope and a love I'd never felt before.

Months later, I met my second husband, "Chad." He lived in Las Vegas but had come home to visit his family. I thought that was exciting and became even more intrigued. After several weeks he asked me if I'd like to go back to Vegas with him, and I said yes. Why not? I had nothing to lose.

I left Brandon with Debbie until Chad and I could get a place together. Somehow Darren found out and took Brandon from Debbie. I filed for divorce, and Darren filed for custody of Brandon. Both were granted. Without the money to fight for Brandon, I returned to Vegas and got married.

When my second son Chuckie came, it was a hard delivery. In labor for twenty-seven hours and hemorrhaging, I needed a blood transfusion. It was another bittersweet time. Enamored with Chuckie, but missing Brandon, Chad and I moved back to Columbus, went to court, and lost the first round, but won back custody of Brandon on appeal. It was all a power trip with Darren. He didn't really care about his son; he never wanted him. But he loved the control.

Chad and I rented a house and started a good life with Brandon and Chuckie. We worked for Mom and Dad in the jewelry business. When business slowed down, I started waitressing, and Chad continued to work for my parents.

Drinking one night with the girls from work because Chad was out of town on business with Dad, I was feeling no pain by the time Chad got home. He was by no means an abusive man, but shoved me because we were arguing. Soon after the fight, I developed a terrible headache and ended up at Urgent Care. I was then rushed to a hospital for further tests, where I received the scariest diagnosis of my life. It would test all the strength I had left.

Chapter 5

Discovering Courage

"When life gives you a hundred reasons to cry,
show life that you have a thousand reasons to smile."
Author Unknown

It took three days in the hospital before we learned the truth. What was initially thought to be a brain aneurism ended up being a brain tumor on the right sight of my head that could have been there for fifteen years or more. Because it was pressing into my motor nerves, I would have been paralyzed within two years if it hadn't been discovered. Without surgery, I would have no more than ten years to live.

I was released from the hospital the next day and told to go home and rest. The doctor wanted to do the surgery right away, but I had to work one more month to be covered by insurance. Waitressing at Bob Evans restaurant proved to be harder than I expected, as I tried to keep my mind off of this life-changing news. When I started to experience seizures, I'd sit in the break room for a few minutes with a cold towel on the back of my neck and then return to waiting tables. This went on for close to forty days, until I was insured.

A day or so before surgery, I had an angiogram. A small incision was made on my inner thigh and a wire was inserted. Dye was shot into the area of the tumor, which in my case caused my eyes to shut until they were pried open again. It was frightening.

The night before surgery, my family took turns coming into my room to wish me well. It was unsettling, because it felt like they were saying their goodbyes.

My doctor, a remarkable surgeon, came to talk. He sat on the edge of my bed, stroked my hair, and wished he didn't have to shave my head. He was very kind and comforting, and all the fear left me.

The day after surgery, with a large drainage bag hanging off the side of my head, I remember trying to wheel myself down the hall for a cigarette, but I was too weak. During my stay, we had a good sized earthquake in Columbus. Chad said he'd check on things down the hall, but I told him he wasn't going without me. So off we went with my IV pole and tubes in hand. We got to the elevator and realized the doors automatically stayed closed during emergencies, so it was back to the room. We laughed, although nervously.

I was out of the hospital in nine days and recovered well. There seemed to be no complications, until I became ill about a month later. At the emergency room, they said I had bronchitis and sent me home. Chad took me again hours later, because I was getting worse. This time, I was diagnosed with a viral infection and sent home again. By the fourth try, he refused to take me home until they found out what was really wrong. My fever rose to 105 degrees, so they packed me in ice in the emergency room. A day later, I was diagnosed with pneumonia, which I'd probably gotten from smoking the night before surgery and was warned not to do.

For financial reasons, we had decided to move back to Vegas when the jewelry business slowed down. So we packed up the boys and headed "home." It was early October 1980. We'd rented a condo, and I'd gotten a great job dealing poker at the Imperial Palace on the strip across from Caesar's Palace. It was beautiful, and I was making great money.

I remember dealing to Redd Foxx, a stand-up comedian and star of the 70s TV series, Sanford and Son. He was playing seven-card stud and not doing well. It was a low-limit game, but every time I'd deal to him, he'd lose the hand. When he finally got up to leave, he asked me if I had a dog. When I answered no, he quipped "When you get one, I hope it dies." Everyone laughed. I thought it was rude and distasteful.

Chad went to Lake Tahoe to play in some tournaments, and I stayed home and worked. I got an unexpected call a few days after my yearly woman's exam. This time it was cervical cancer. A hysterectomy was scheduled, which hit me harder than news of the cancer. I wanted more children, but it wasn't to be. It was a sad and scary time for me.

The surgery went well. I was in the hospital for five days, but as usual, not without excitement. There was a fire in the hospital. By the time Chad got down the hall, the emergency doors had shut automatically. We sat in the room and waited for the drama to pass.

By April 1981, our lives started to settle down, when we noticed the boys weren't running around and having their usual fun. The doctor diagnosed them with hepatitis A, probably contracted at their daycare center from improper sanitation. About a week later, Chad started acting lethargic and then turned yellow. He spent five days in the hospital, where his jaundice worsened. The day he got home, I came down with the virus and was admitted to the hospital, but for only three days. Discouraged and homesick, we decided to pack up and move back to Columbus.

Still weak from hepatitis, we took turns driving, four hours at a time. It was a hard cross-country trip, but thank God, the boys endured and began to thrive again. We lived with Chad's mom, and I started working at a poker club in town where Chad played.

We then bought a farm in southern Ohio and started over. The boys loved it. We had a pony named Pickles. To make money, Chad raised worms called Alabama Jumpers to sell to wholesale bait stores. When our washer and dryer broke, we opened a pizza business at home in the empty laundry room. It went well for a while. We paid neighborhood kids to deliver pizza on their bikes but still had to make the long commute back and forth to Columbus to deal poker.

Some friends owned a bar across the street from the poker club, so we usually ended up there several nights a week after work. That's when we started to drink more. I wish I could explain why I cheated with one of the guys from the club. Not long after Chad found out, he cheated on me with a dancer. Our marriage unraveled.

It's hard to believe, but sometime in the early 1980s, I had a nervous breakdown *after* the brain tumor, pneumonia, cancer, and hepatitis A, and all within about a year and a half. We don't know how much strength we truly have until we're put to the test. We may not understand all we're going through or all that's happened to us, but we should never give up. I've done my best to live by these words.

Still, I did something that took a huge toll on my sons and grieves me to this day. I made a decision in 1982 that I'll regret until the day I die. To make ends meet, I had always worked two jobs since divorcing Darren, because he refused to pay child support. I decided that since my two sons were with the sitter more than they were with me, they would be better off with their dads. I loved both my sons very much. I just wanted the best for them. I really believed I was giving them a better chance at a good life.

I didn't think of the lasting, long-term effects nor of the terrible price we would all pay later on. Chuckie had a pretty good life with his dad, but Brandon didn't fare as well. His dad was cold and harsh and raised him to "do as I say, not as I do." Brandon's "stepmoms" didn't treat him much better. He was raised without the loving nurture and encouragement he deserved. I know now he felt unloved, confused, fearful, and helpless to do much about his circumstances.

"Forgiveness doesn't change the past, but it does enlarge the future." (Paul Boese)

I am learning to forgive myself, and I pray someday that both my sons forgive me. In my heart of hearts, my intentions were never to hurt them. I always wanted to be a good mother, but I just couldn't find my way.

Chapter 6

Moving On, Not Up

"Choices are the hinges of destiny."
Edwin Markham, Pythagoras

In the fall of 1983, my parents opened a steakhouse and lounge, and I worked for them as a waitress. Debbie was the kitchen manager, at least as much as she was allowed to be. Featured on a weekly television magazine show that highlighted local commerce, we had all the who's who in town dining there, and business was booming.

The steakhouse had a huge salad and spud bar, and you could grill your own steaks and garlic bread. Along with a banquet room, there was a Hawaiian-themed lounge downstairs and a country lounge designed like an old western saloon upstairs, both with live entertainment. It was Mom's idea. She had a wonderful imagination and was talented and creative.

The business did quite well for about a year and a half. But within the first year we all began to drink more. We'd drink at lunch and then sneak drinks while we were working. After the dining room closed, we'd drink in the lounge. Things became intense, when I became general manager. We were all putting in eighty hours a week or better, arriving early to clean, opening at 11 o'clock for lunch, and staying till closing. Everyone felt the stress. We were overworked and overwhelmed, and the drinking didn't help.

Then the harassment started. We guessed some of the local bigwigs felt threatened by our success. There'd be sudden police raids on Friday nights. Everyone was ordered outside, which disrupted business and upset our customers. This happened over and over again for months.

My parents had poured their hearts and souls into the restaurant, but eventually had to file for bankruptcy. Along with Mom's beautifully carved stand-up tables in the lounge, the hand-carved bars, and those amazing wall murals, they lost their house and just about everything else.

By this time, I'd learned how to function in a drunken stupor, as well as manage my professional life the "day after." Under the stress of working eighty to ninety hours a week, I began to snort cocaine regularly and never slowed down on the drinking. A friend would conveniently drop by the bar several times a week with extra cocaine or crack. I lost about thirty pounds.

One night, I went out drinking alone and met a guy named Juan. He was good looking and flashed money around. One thing led to another, and we started dating. Before I knew it, I was "in love." When I learned he was a major drug dealer from up north, it didn't matter, because I didn't matter.

I started "muling" cocaine from Florida to northern Ohio for Juan. Muling is equivalent to smuggling. I made regular trips, and they were exciting, although I could have gotten busted many times. Once, in an airport in Tennessee, I had just claimed my baggage (with cocaine inside) when I saw drug-sniffing dogs headed towards the luggage carrier as I walked out.

Another time, I drove a dual-tank pickup truck so I'd have double the gas, which meant less stops. At the Florida-Georgia border, the roads were slick with rain, and I fishtailed into a shallow ditch and couldn't get out. I had a suitcase full of cocaine on the floorboard of the front passenger side and was wearing a SWAT hat that I'd gotten when they'd raided a house and busted Juan just a few weeks before. I was making this trip to pay the lawyer.

While I tried to figure out what to do next (no cell phones back then), a highway patrol car pulled up. Because of the heavy rain, the officer got out of his cruiser and into the front seat with me. As he wrote down details, I was sweating bullets. I denied knowing that it was illegal to wear a SWAT hat unless I was an officer and told him my boyfriend was with the police back in Ohio. Thank God he didn't ask me Juan's badge number.

He'd called for a wrecker and said he'd follow me to the first gas station in Georgia to be sure I made it. I thought it might be a set up, so I didn't breathe until I finally pulled out of that gas station and was back on the road. If that wasn't enough, a few hours later I stopped to get something to drink and heard someone talking about the Nighthawks, a drug task force in Georgia that travels the highways from 9:00 p.m. to 9:00 a.m. So I got a motel room for the night and headed out at 9:01 a.m. I made quite a few more trips but never got caught.

When Juan and I started getting high on our supply, things got worse between us. Breaking this number-one rule of drug dealers was our downfall. Juan became more violent and abusive with me and more suspicious of everyone else.

Because I just wanted to feel loved again, I hooked up with one of Juan's boys. When Juan found out, he and another girl dragged me out of bed naked and beat me for hours, taking turns when they got tired. When they finished, I threw a blanket around me and started walking down the road to nowhere. Juan chased me down in his car, put me next to him in the front seat, and acted like everything was okay. So bloodied and swollen that I couldn't see or speak, I left with him. What else could I do?

Another night, we'd gone to collect drug money, and I got impatient waiting in the car, so I followed Juan into an apartment. While I tried to persuade Juan to leave, I was blindsided by someone with brass knuckles. When Juan did nothing, I ran out to the car in a blind rage, my face wet with blood from a bone protruding at my temple.

I tried to drive forward and hit a car, then backed up and hit another. I was too delirious to figure out how to get out of the parking lot, but finally escaped to an old farmhouse, where an elderly couple called for an ambulance. After eighteen stitches in my head and face, we were given a motel room by the county. That's God's mercy. I just didn't realize it at the time.

Even after all that had gone on that night, Juan sexually abused me. It didn't matter that my head was exploding in pain, as long as he got what he wanted. Aware of what he was capable of, he knew I'd never say no. When abuse is the norm, you become so desensitized to pain and violence that you just accept it to the point of welcoming death. Still, I started to see Juan for who he really was.

Another time, Juan threw me down a flight of stairs. To escape the violence, I kicked my way into a closed restaurant next door, failed to break the front window with a fire extinguisher to get out, and finally ran for my life through the back door. Desperate and petrified that he'd follow me, I found a bridge and was ready to jump, when the cops arrived. One officer tried to talk me down before another jerked me to the ground, and I was taken to the hospital . . . again.

This time I had cracked ribs and a fractured neck. I was too scared to tell them what Juan had done; I was in his hometown. I was waiting with a police officer for transport to a psychiatric facility for evaluation, when the hospital fire alarm went off. The officer went one way to check it out, and I went the other, neck brace and all. I ran as fast as I could through the woods until I found a boy delivering early morning papers and talked him into letting me borrow his bike, which I later left at a restaurant.

With no money and nowhere to go, I went back to Juan. As his drug habit increased, he resorted to double crossing his dealers and suppliers. Without money for drugs, he forced me to sell my body to make up the deficit. He'd traffick me from northern Ohio, to Texas, to Mexico. It was terrifying to be part of a drug deal, expected to do whatever I was told, but I knew Juan would make good on his threats to destroy me. He'd proven that to me time and again.

I didn't know if I'd make it out of Mexico alive. I recall an incident when I was the only woman in a backyard with dozens of men. Juan paired me with a young man and then, without warning, jerked me out of bed and dragged me outside, screaming at me in front of the other men. I had no idea why Juan was enraged. It was extremely degrading.

Wherever we went, I was in constant fear and on high alert. I had learned to live on very little sleep and even less food. I'd be left by strange men in motel rooms with no money, no car, and no way to fend for myself. I knew staying with Juan meant eventual death. When a "new girl" entered the picture, I returned to Columbus, but Juan continued to plague me at all hours of the night no matter where I lived or worked. He always found me somehow.

I'd distanced myself from Juan for about a year and was living with my new boyfriend, Carl, when Juan showed up one night, asking me to take a Mexican general to a motel and wait for him there. Afraid to say no, I talked Carl into going with us. Once there, Juan's plans for me became apparent when Carl was asked to leave. Remarkably, I found the courage to leave with him.

Thank God that, in the end, Juan just quit showing up. Considering how he lived his life and conducted his business, I doubt he survived, though I've wondered over the years what became of him.

Chapter 7

Welcome to Hell

"While I thought that I was learning how to live,
I have been learning how to die."
Leonardo Da Vinci

When I started working at a bar on the west side of town, I thought I'd found the job of my dreams. The owners, a married couple named Ed and Sandy, were good to me. We drank all day, and the patrons turned me onto drugs—usually cocaine, crack, or crystal meth.

The money was great, but my life spiraled out of control. Miserable without my children, I still had no way of caring for them as they deserved. I had learned to cope with my pain by staying in a drunken, drug-crazed state of mind. I lived in motel rooms. Rather than rent an apartment, I hoarded my hard-earned money for drugs. When Ed and Sandy parked their new RV at the bar, it became my new home. We worked long, hard hours six days a week, and most Sundays, took the RV to Hamilton, Ohio, simply to visit a bar the owners liked.

That's where I met my third husband, "Tony." He was a commercial painter/sub-contractor. Within eight months, we were living together, working hard all day, and often drinking all night and on weekends.

My criminal record grew with thirty days in jail, when I got an OMVI ticket for drinking and driving. Jail time wasn't what I expected; I actually made new "friends" there, but got worse when I got out. While on probation, a girl pressed charges against me for beating her up, and I ended up behind bars for almost six months.

When I got out, I wanted to do right but didn't know how. Tony and I got married right away; we had our reception at a neighborhood bar with "wedding pizza" instead of cake. (Pizza goes better with beer, right?)

At that point, I couldn't drink without smoking crack. Tony loved me despite my consuming drug habit, but he was getting in the way of my getting high. What did I need true love for anyway? I found a new love, crack. We divorced a short time later.

When Ed and Sandy were forced to sell their bar and bought another, I followed right behind them. Unlike their first bar, this was small, and the money was bad. For a short time, I rented a room from a regular customer, but it didn't work out. Next, I found an apartment right down from the bar and moved from my rented room by pushing a shopping-cartful of my belongings in the snow. Carl moved in with me, and I continued to roll with the punches (no pun intended), never stopping long enough to wonder why life was so hard.

A year or so later, while working one night, Juan showed up. Terrified, I approached him and said hello. By his sinister grin and the tone of his voice, I knew I had to do whatever he wanted—which was to get him drugs, of course. I knew right where to get them, so I made some lame excuse and took off with Juan. This kind of thing went on for a while, before he disappeared altogether.

When Carl became abusive, I was able to get away, but because of my crack addiction, I fell deeper into the darkness. I was finished with life and decided hell could have me. After all, I'd made my home there for years.

On a mission to buy my "last meal" of steak, salad, and bread and butter, along with a bottle of aspirin, which I planned to kill myself with after my meal, I walked the local grocery store wishing I could just lie down and die. I stuffed a bag of salad and the steak under my shirt and the aspirins in my pocket, but on my way to the register I felt guilty, turned around, and returned the good steak, then went over to the marked-down section and picked out a cheap one.

At the register, I paid for the bread and butter and was headed for the door, when a security guard asked me to step into the store office. When the guard and a manager questioned me, I simply told them my plans and sat waiting to be arrested for shoplifting. Miraculously, the manager said that if I could find someone to come and get me, he'd let me go without pressing charges. Perhaps it was out of pity, as I was a mere one hundred pounds by then. Amazing!

I immediately called Sandy, and while waiting for her to pick me up, thought, *"Thank God, no jail time. Things are looking up."* Sandy bought me bread and bologna at the local carryout, and then wanted to stop at the bar before taking me home. The joke was on me, when Sandy "shared" what happened with several people drinking around the bar. One guy said, "You're so stupid, you don't even know how to kill yourself right," and then went on laughing with the rest of them.

After that, I stayed drunk every day. No longer a functioning drug addict, I lost my job and then my apartment. I missed my sons terribly, thought of them often, and pictured them happy and having fun with their dads, but was too busy trying to survive my personal hell to do more.

Jim and Tom, guys a few doors down, offered to let me sleep on their couch until I could find somewhere else to go. Pretty soon, we were smoking crack together and using each other for whatever we needed. Once I wore out my welcome, I got the "bright idea" of prostituting myself. It just seemed like another way to survive. Jim gave me a reprieve and let me live there another month, because I could still pay some rent. I stayed until the night I got busted.

I was on my usual *ho stroll* (I think they call it their *track* now). I'd been working several hours when an undercover cop approached by car. He was working the area that night, but I didn't recognize him. Before I knew it, I was busted for solicitation. I escaped drug charges by sneaking my crack pipe out of my back pocket and stuffing it into his seat.

I was about to be released after six days in the Franklin County jail, but because of an outstanding warrant from another county, I was

31

transported from one jail to another. Thank God Debbie got Mom and Dad to bail me out. I was facing a year in prison for probation violation and an outstanding five-hundred-dollar fine.

When Dad started his public tongue-lashing, I told the sheriff to take me to prison, preferring the year in jail to further humiliation. Then things calmed down. But, after an unpleasant drive to Mom and Dad's, I couldn't wait to get back to the west side and threatened to hitchhike there if I didn't get a ride. I really needed a fix.

Debbie knew one way or another I'd find a way back, so she gave in, but there was nothing to come back to. Jim had moved out, and Ed and Sandy's wasn't an option. When some of the local dealers I knew offered me a place to stay at their crack house, I thought things were looking up again. I'd have a place to stay and maybe some free drugs. I couldn't have been more wrong. I thought I knew evil, but never this kind. My nightmares got worse than I could have ever imagined, my hell even hotter.

Physical and sexual abuse came daily, but not food. I ate only when fed and slept a few hours at a time. I'd distract convenient-store cashiers while my captors stuffed two or three hot dogs down their throats and then walked calmly out, leaving me there, hungry. I slept on the floor with no blanket or pillow. I had no toothbrush and no change of clothes for months, so I took showers with my clothes on. There are no words for the depths of depravity I witnessed and experienced, things too debasing to speak out loud, things that only God knows about.

Maybe I didn't know who I was in the first place, but whatever sense of self I'd managed to make due was long gone. Once the damage began, the "real me" was lost, beaten out of me till I was a shell of a person. I had spent my life being whatever anyone else wanted me to be. Without encouragement, support, and proper treatment, the trauma of abuse at an early age made me at high risk for the alcohol and drug addiction and other mental health issues that became my lifestyle.

In an emotional coma, but still totally aware of everything happening to me and around me, I felt helpless and hopeless. With no respect, no values, no morals, no fear, no life, I was totally void of human emotion. Death seemed a valid option.

Incredibly, I found myself on the street when, after several months, the dealers I "lived with" were evicted. I called Mom. Though I couldn't bear her lecturing, who could blame her for it? She'd bailed me out of countless messes and tried to help me as best she could. I knew she was tired of it and tired of me. I was tired of me, too.

I asked Mom to call Debbie, who asked me to find somewhere to go until her husband Chet picked me up after work that afternoon. I had no reason or capacity to hope for more than a place to rest and to plan my next move. I realized I was fully responsible for all the terrible life choices I'd made and had only worsened my circumstances by my sinful responses to the damage that began at an early age. I had no one to blame but myself for most of my pain and suffering.

They say that a man all wrapped up in himself makes a pretty small package. I guess that was me. I was so accustomed to wallowing in self-pity that it became my world. I could've reached out for help, but I never once took an honest look at my life. If I had, I could've saved my sons, my family, and myself years of heartache. But change was coming. I was about to meet the greatest Person in my life.

Chapter 8

Metamorphosis

"Just when the caterpillar thought life was over,
she became a beautiful butterfly."
Mumsgather

Chet picked me up as planned, and we drove towards southern Ohio, where he and my sister Debbie lived. I don't remember a lot about the drive except the long, winding road that led up to their house. Their beautiful resort community had hillsides strewn with all sorts of A-frame style homes and a big lake for fishing and boating. The closer we got, the stranger I felt.

It was January 4, 1994. The snow was several inches deep and covered the trees lining both sides of the road, limbs sagging, heavy from the weight. This created a covered highway, as if you were driving into a cocoon. The most wonderful feeling coursed through my body. I had no clue what it was, but I sure didn't want it to stop

We pulled up to their beautiful A-frame, and I was awestruck. Their home was set into the side of a hill. Glass covered the front, and there were two large decks, one upper and one lower. You could sit on either deck, see out onto the lake, and watch deer running through the surrounding woods. It was the coolest place I'd ever seen. When we entered the house, the strange feeling returned. It was so surreal, so mesmerizing; it almost left me speechless. Several months later, I realized that I had entered the peace of God.

It was so good to be with Debbie, who I hadn't seen for a year or two by then. I'd gotten into the habit of avoiding my family during my "dark days," not wanting to burden them. Frankly, I didn't know what to say anymore. I hadn't been normal for so many years that it didn't seem right to communicate. I'd been "living in a cave" without real human interaction for so long, that it was hard to have a normal conversation. In fact, I was so uncomfortable in my own skin that just trying to be normal was agonizing. I could barely make eye contact.

Debbie welcomed me with open arms, an open heart, and an open home. I thank God for her every day. She was always in my corner. Mom would have let me stay with her too, but it wouldn't have been the same. With Debbie, for the first time in I don't know how many years, I felt a tiny hint of love. Deprived for so long, I didn't know how to handle it.

Chet and Debbie went to bed, leaving me to "sleep" downstairs. It seemed unimaginable that I'd left the crack house just the day before. I was used to years of non-stop action into the wee hours of the morning, seven days a week. There was always something going on— noisy people doing God-knows-what abusive thing—so that even if I'd wanted to sleep, I couldn't.

Late into the night, I'd gone into their kitchen, looked in their pantry, and quietly opened all the cabinet doors. I just sat there and stared at all the food on the shelves. I couldn't get over how many cans and boxes there were; it was unbelievable. I hadn't seen that much food for almost a decade. As ridiculous as that sounds, when you've been at the mercy of strangers to feed you, it's not so hard to imagine. I could take a can of chili, uncooked, and make it last almost a week. It's amazing what you can endure to survive. I eventually closed all the cabinet doors and went back to try and get some sleep.

Before long, I heard Debbie get up, and joined her in the kitchen for coffee and small talk. It was uncomfortable and comforting at the same time. Was this really happening? Was I really in a normal home with a family member? Were Debbie and I together again? Yes, yes, yes, and it was wonderful!

Just when I dared to let myself relax, Debbie asked me two remarkable questions, "Do you want to be saved? Will you say the salvation prayer and ask Jesus into your heart?" Without hesitation, I said yes to both.

Looking back, Mom, Debbie, and my cousin Donna had all tried to get me to turn to God years before, but I didn't want any part of it. I'd been mad at God most of my life because of the things I'd gone through. How could a good God let my dad die a month before I was born? What about all the other bad things that had happened to me?

Years later, I realized it wasn't God who hurt me, but the devil. We have a loving God who wants only the best for His children. The devil wants to destroy us because he hates God. He knows if we come through our trials, we'll "live to tell" and help others turn to the Lord.

We went in and sat down on her couch, Debbie took me by the hand, and we prayed. It was just a short, simple prayer, "Jesus, I repent of all my sins. Come into my heart, wash me white as snow, and help me to live for You always."

Something subtle changed in me. I couldn't tell what it was, but I knew it was good. Debbie showed me the Scripture for the day on her inspirational table calendar. It said, *"I will turn your sorrow into joy."* (John 16:20) She floated all over the kitchen as she made more coffee and wiped the counter. I didn't realize that inside, she was celebrating the return of the prodigal daughter. Then she had me call Mom. It was sweet.

When things had calmed down later that evening, I realized something truly amazing had happened. I had no craving whatsoever for drugs or alcohol. Weeks, even months passed, and I never experienced one withdrawal symptom. No nausea, no headaches, no rehab, no AA meetings. I'd been an alcoholic for almost thirty years and an addict for almost fourteen. How could this be? How could I start a prayer as a drug-addicted alcoholic, and finish totally different, delivered, set free, at peace? Only the power of God explains it. He had done a miracle in me. Suddenly! Instantly!

I'd never known true peace before. The feeling was unfamiliar, but I liked it. Debbie and I would sit for hours, and she'd teach me all kinds of things about God. In fact, she gave me my first Bible. It was good to be with her—whether buying groceries, shopping at the thrift store, or going out to lunch—and I started to feel good inside. Debbie always had this way of making me feel at home, no matter what was going on. I felt safe and full of hope.

I came to realize that she'd never given up on me. She'd prayed for me every day and had others praying, too. Even Mom had never stopped praying, though I know I gave her enough reason to hate me. Without these faithful prayer warriors, I wouldn't have made it. Debbie even had a "re-birthday" party for me, since I was now born again. It was wonderful!

Most of us know the story of the butterfly. It starts out as an ugly worm, but then enters a new phase of life. It becomes very still for a while, and then finds a limb or the backside of a leaf, and slowly starts spinning a silk cocoon, totally encasing itself. The miracle starts to happen in this quiet, still place. In time, the cocoon cracks open, and suddenly, a beautiful, one-of-a-kind butterfly emerges. It's amazing to see the total transformation and the parallel to our lives. A worm suddenly transformed into a butterfly with vividly colored wings, as if an artist painted a masterpiece. That's how salvation happens. When we surrender our hearts to God, He makes us new creatures in Christ. *"Old things are passed away, and all things become brand new."* (2 Corinthians 5:17) The old self is dead, the new, alive in Him.

It's up to us to believe and receive. I did. I thought I was too far gone for God, or anyone else, to want me or see anything good in me. I thank Him every day for saving my life and delivering me instantly from the drugs, alcohol, and cigarettes. He wants to bless, deliver, and heal you too, if you'll let Him. What have you got to lose? *"Whom the Son sets free is free indeed."* (John 8:36) You too can spread your wings and fly.

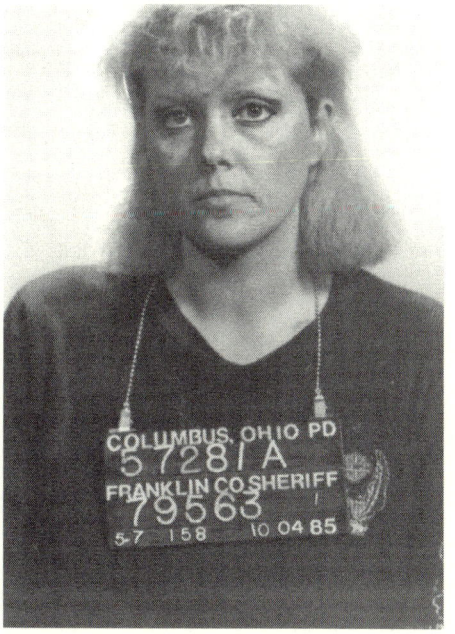

Chapter 9

Back into Darkness

"Darkness is only driven out with light,
not more darkness."
Martin Luther King, Jr.

After four months at Debbie's, Mom and my sister Carrie suggested I move out and get a job. They felt Debbie and Chet had taken care of me long enough and thought I should start taking care of myself. Debbie urged me not go. She knew it was too soon. I'd only been a Christian for a few months and wasn't strong enough to make it on my own without lots of support and mentoring. But I felt guilty staying at Debbie and Chet's, so I moved out.

Carrie had gotten me a job at a restaurant in a small town nearby and had arranged for me to live with one of the girls who worked there. Our small apartment was above a store and had no windows, which bothered me, but I thought this was a good start. My roommate Donna was easy to get along with, and I began waitressing right away. We'd get pizza on weekends, watch movies, and talk about God. I made good money and did the right thing for several months, but without a church, I started to slip away.

Restless one night, I walked to the bar a few doors down, Bible in hand, and ordered a Coke—uncomfortable and unusual behavior, especially for me. I struck up a conversation with a guy, who later that night, decided to give his heart to the Lord. I thought, "Wow, how easy!" So as my nightly ritual, I'd go to the bar and "get people saved."

Several weeks and souls later, I was doing my thing when someone offered to buy me a beer. Initially, I said, "No, thank you," but my resolve was eventually worn down. I figured there couldn't be any harm in just one beer. Pretty soon, I had a few more. Before you knew it, I had a beer in one hand and a Bible in the other. I thought I was still doing okay, because I was still "saving souls" several nights a week.

Inevitably, the old me emerged, and I was back to being a full-blown alcoholic, at bars almost every night, but without my Bible. My roommate Donna and I drifted apart. She battled her own demons, and I didn't take the time to have deep conversations. Later, I found a whole lot of wine bottles in a closet. Donna hid her alcoholism well. Unfortunately, four years later, she killed herself. I wish I would have been caring enough to see her problems, but I was fighting my own war.

Someone offered me cocaine one night, opening the door to darkness I thought had been closed for good. Soon, I was drinking more, doing cocaine regularly, and slowly shutting out my family again. I thought the less they knew, the better off I was. I never realized how selfish I was being. I remember shortly after being saved, Mom had heard on the six o'clock news of a woman's body being found on the west side. She'd waited up to watch the eleven o'clock news to make sure it wasn't me.

About two months later I met a guy, who turned out to be a worse alcoholic than I was, and moved in with him. I lived with Jerry for three or four months, Things got bad quickly, when he lost his job and began drinking more. Private and distant, he was neither affectionate nor a conversationalist. We both smoked crack, but the old addict in me didn't want to share, so I'd always hide and do mine. He got worse and I got worse. It was the same old song. I was my own worst enemy.

After several months of arguing, Jerry told me to leave. Then I got mad at my boss at the restaurant, told him off, and quit. No job, no car, no home . . . again! After a few weeks, I got a low paying job at a little diner in town and was somehow able to get a small, two-room apartment, furnished with a mattress on the floor and a folding lawn chair. There was no television or radio.

My habit got worse, and the crack consumed me again. I remember waking up and thinking, *What's the use? There's absolutely no purpose to my life, no reason to even wake up.* As I look back now, that was the second-worst feeling I had during my addiction.

Sometimes I'd get up my nerve and call Debbie again, but only every six months or so. Without fail, she'd offer words of encouragement and love; she never lectured me or put me down. That's why I loved her so much.

In time, I couldn't pay rent. I'd lost my job again, and any money I did have went for drugs and beer, nothing else. I didn't even care if I ate. I had no choice but to make the dreaded call to my parents, but thank God, they let me stay with them. Amazingly, God delivered me from the drugs and alcohol again. I regained my strength, got another job waitressing, and even found a church.

Then I prayed for a car with a good stereo and sunroof that would cost only five hundred dollars, because that was all the money I'd saved. I found one for eight hundred dollars. The sunroof had been installed the year before for the owner's daughter, and of course, it had a great stereo. I'd forgotten to pray about the color. It was a bright, metallic green, but hey, it was wheels. When it came time to buy, my five hundred dollars was accepted. What a miracle!

Back with God, working again, and making good money, I was able to get out of debt. But I was getting restless, so it was back to the bars. I'd lost my taste for beer, but I was lonely. Next, I decided it was time to get my own place. Soon, I was smoking crack every night. This roller coaster went on for several more years. I'd hit the crack pipe, read Scriptures, and preach.

The pattern continued. I met a guy who said I was a diamond in the rough. I thought that was sweet, so we began dating. When I fell on a wet floor and shattered my elbow, he wasn't too compassionate with me, and turned out to be quite an alcoholic, so that relationship didn't last. I had to have surgery to put a pin in my elbow, and then surgery again about five months later, because it didn't heal right. There were always physical problems with me, but God brought me through every one of them.

Then I met a construction worker named "Tim," who'd come in for lunch. All it took this time was a dozen roses. We moved in together two months later, and I became stepmom to his three teenage kids. Meanwhile, I'd quit the restaurant and went to work picking and packing lingerie orders. To get the job, I'd lied on my application about my prior convictions.

Within a month, I found myself being escorted to Personnel by two burly security guards. They made a big scene in front of everyone on the way there, sat me in a chair, interrogated me for half an hour about my prostitution, and made another big scene when they walked me out of the building. I was trying to do right by getting a job, but it turned out wrong.

When I went to the doctor for my yearly checkup, they found a lump. I later had surgery to remove the benign tumor, and everything was fine. But I'd decided it was time to get out of Dodge. We moved to a trailer in southern Ohio, where I thought things would be better. After all, we were out of town, a good hour and a half from my drug dealers.

Different location, same problems. We'd get drunk and fight. The kids were older and acted up a lot. The stress was unbearable, and I made every excuse to take off. I'd stagger over to busy Interstate 23 and thumb to Columbus to get my drugs. It was crazy.

That's the effect I had on people; I could drive anyone crazy. I had learned over the years how to drive everyone away, especially those I loved. It was my way of protecting myself, but it also kept everyone out. Out of my life and out of my heart. I didn't want this to happen, but I didn't know how to stop the madness. A storm was always brewing in me. I was fighting my own private war, and I was defenseless. I couldn't win, but I couldn't give up either.

Chapter 10

"Touched by an Angel"

"Angels deliver fate to our doorstep . . .
and anywhere else it is needed."
Jessi Lane Adams

There was one particular night like no other. It started out with my usual routine. Have some fun, get drunk, start a fight, justify my actions, hide my guilt, and head for Columbus. As I made my way to Route 23, stumbling through the streets, I noticed a car slow down. The driver, a black guy, asked me if I needed help. I said, "Yeah, you can give me a ride to Columbus." To my amazement, he said okay. The next thing I knew, we were sitting at my dealer's house, smoking crack.

I didn't pay much attention to him after that; I was too busy getting high. Every now and then I'd throw him a kibble (tiny bit of crack). I'd look over later, and it would be gone, but I never saw him smoke it; he never had a stem. After a few hours, I was out of dope and out of money. My driver asked me if I was ready to go, I said yes, and we left. I'd usually beg or bargain for more dope, but not this time. I just got in the car, and we headed home.

I don't recall if we even talked on the ride, but I'll never forget what happened next! I didn't want Tim to see me getting out of the car, so we stopped a block from my trailer. I was about to get out when the driver said, "I like your cross." I'd gotten the special necklace shortly after being saved. It depicts Jesus on the cross at Mount Calvary. I thanked him and then asked him his name.

He calmly explained, "My name is not important. I'm an angel sent by God to help you, because you were supposed to die tonight." I stared at him in a daze, then got out of the car and headed toward the trailer. When I turned quickly back, the car was nowhere in sight. By then, it was early morning, May 15, 1998. I'll remember that date forever!

When I got home, all hell broke loose. Tim was enraged and drinking. His kids took turns badgering me with their remarks. I simply went to our bedroom and began watching television. The angel encounter left me speechless. I couldn't even think. It was a good thing too, because the torture went on all day.

In shock, I didn't speak for several days. God's peace and presence put me in a profound state of awe and wonder. Praise God for the angel He sent! Tim and his children moved out shortly afterwards. I was trying to make it on my own, but had no money to live on. I decided to do something about it.

I calmly went through the trailer and got all the pills I could find, took them all at once, and kept drinking. I wrote goodbye letters to my sons and family and called my son Brandon in Columbus. Whatever I said must have scared him, because he called for help.

I'd tried to commit suicide dozens of times since I was thirteen, but this time I felt completely at peace; the steps to suicide felt natural. This false peace from the devil was meant to make sure I'd succeed and finally die. I woke up in the emergency room as they were pumping my stomach. It was terrible. I was so out of it that I tried to cause trouble with the doctors and nurses to get out of there. When they threatened me with arrest, I calmed down. Mom, Dad, and Brandon were my only visitors.

When I heard, "We're losing her, her blood pressure is seventy over forty," it got my attention. Would I choose to die or fight and live? Was this my last chance to live for God and change once and for all?

When I was released, Dad and Mom tried to persuade me to go home with them, but I insisted they take me back to my trailer. While I was gone, Tim and his kids had taken all they wanted and left. The place was trashed. All I could do was sit and stare at the mess. I used my neighbor's phone to call Debbie, and once again, she sent Chet to help me gather my stuff and return with him. So, it was back to square one.

Debbie insisted, at God's prompting, that I stay with her for at least forty days. I started going to church, and during prayer, the pastor saw a glow around my mid-section and said God was healing me. This was amazing, because the doctors had told me to see a specialist due to the damage done to my kidneys and liver from the suicide attempt. God was drawing a line in the sand and wanted me to decide if I was in our out with Him. So I made up my mind once and for all to go all the way with God. It was time to get right or get left (behind).

By October 1998, I had gotten another waitressing job, and within a few months I was able to get my own place again. It was the cutest loft apartment I'd ever seen; it even had a garage. I loved it. I was making good money, was debt free, living a good life, and at peace.

I found a church a few miles down the road called The Barn. It had burlap sacks for curtains and was literally in a barn made of natural wood. I loved it there. My pastor and his wife were so kind, and the praise and worship and preaching were alive and uplifting. It was my home church for three years, but there would be a price to pay for my freedom.

Chapter 11

Sleeping with the Enemy

"How many years can some people exist
before they're allowed to be free?"
Bob Dylan

What an awesome and powerful God we serve! He not only delivered me once from years of drug abuse and alcoholism, but He did it three times . . . instantly, with no drug rehab, no withdrawal. I was really beginning to grow.

I was also beginning to enjoy life. I had a great home, a great job, and a great church. I was sure the dark ugliness I'd known was long behind me, and it gave me peace. I was blissfully unaware of what lay ahead.

I began to notice a handsome man at church. I would see "Stan" at every Sunday morning and Sunday night service. He was quiet and always alone, but seemed to know some of the other church members. One day, I decided to introduce myself. By the end of that service, he had asked me out for coffee.

We began dating, which usually meant we'd talk or watch television at my apartment. Sometimes we'd go out to dinner, and he'd always call. Within six weeks we were married. Only one couple from church warned that I should have waited at least six months to know Stan better. What I did know was that he was a former Oxycontin addict and was living in a shelter when we met. I believed him when he said God had delivered him from his addiction. After all, God had done it for me. Plus, he was in church every Sunday and seemed humble and sincere.

I kept getting the Scripture, *"Unless God builds the house they labor in vain."* I thought this was my confirmation from God to marry, but it was actually a warning. God wasn't building this house, the devil was.

Things started out fine; we both worked and went to church regularly. But within a couple of months, Stan asked me to quit my job, because he didn't want me to work. That was the beginning of his controlling me, but I didn't see it.

Another month passed, and Stan talked me into buying three cell phones to start his home improvement business. Then I had to get two more credit cards. Before long, Stan had walked off his job, sticking me with three credit cards and three cell phones. And to make matters worse, he'd given one of the phones to his daughter, who continually ran up our bill by hundreds of dollars.

By April 2001, just four months after we'd gotten married, Stan stopped going to church and started fishing three or four times a week, often overnight. I was upset at first, and tried to get him back in church or, at least, home more often. Eventually, I welcomed the time alone. I still smoked, and he didn't like it and insisted I sit out in the cold garage. We argued a lot, and he was becoming abusive. Debbie was my only lifeline to peace and support. I'd sneak in calls when I could.

One weekend, Debbie and I attended an out-of-town women's conference. Several hours into the first evening, I had an overwhelming urge to go home. Debbie confirmed it, and we left, arriving at my apartment around dinner time. Stan was startled to see me.

On the way to my bedroom, I noticed a receipt for a pornographic movie and confronted Stan about it. Stan "had no clue" where it had come from. I put the receipt on the dresser and said I would call the next morning to ask about it. Of course by morning, the receipt was gone, and Stan had no idea where it went.

Within days he started abusing me verbally and physically. Stan was the most verbally abusive man I'd ever known and second only to Juan in physical abuse. He loved to get about an inch from my face and scream as loud as he could, calling me every name imaginable. It was a new kind of torment.

I'd sit there and pray silently. When he didn't get a response, he'd get louder or leave. He tried to choke me several times, and raped me violently one night. Wearied and weakened, I'd call Debbie, who encouraged me to keep praying.

Stan had also found a way to withdraw money from our account beyond our balance. The bank required only that the money be re-deposited within a few days of withdrawal. Instead, Stan took the money and partied on Oxycontin. Thank God, the bank didn't hold me responsible.

After almost ten months of hell, I'd taken all I could stand. I had called the police several times, but because we were married, I couldn't get Stan out, and they wouldn't arrest him. I secretly called a domestic violence agency. They told me to change the locks on my door and offered to help me pay for a dissolution of marriage.

Sometime later that week, when Stan took off for his usual partying, I had a locksmith waiting. I put his stuff outside and refused to answer the door when he tried countless times to kick it in and terrorize me. For several weeks, he called me every two minutes for hours on end, but I stood my ground and was finally rid of him.

During this terribly tormenting time, I experienced severe foot pain and would soak both feet on and off all day to ease the discomfort. Stan kept up his insane phone calling to the point that I had to keep my phone off the hook until he finally stopped. He almost broke me, but God was there!

I contacted Debbie for prayer and advice on what I should do next. I had no success finding a job and, with no money, would soon be behind on my rent. I ended up calling my sister Carrie, who thankfully offered to let me stay with her. Praise God, a few weeks later, she and a friend helped me pack up and move. Carrie was kind and understanding, and I settled in comfortably.

I couldn't work because I could barely walk. So I would cook and clean and do Carrie's laundry for my keep. I finally went to see a doctor, who diagnosed me with plantar fasciitis, where the nerve on the bottom of your foot gets inflamed and causes horrific pain. We scheduled surgery on each foot a month apart.

I'd met the pastor of Carrie and Mom's church and started attending. One Sunday, God used me to speak a word of wisdom to the pastor's praise and worship team, something I'd never experienced. They were husband and wife, and the husband instantly confirmed the word. We became quick friends.

About two months later, I got a call from the husband, Ed. He asked me to pray about an important decision he needed to make, and I was prompted to quote Scripture about Abraham, when God told him to go without worrying about where. Ed let out a shout and said he and his wife had been wavering for some time about whether they should leave the church and move to another town, and now they had their answer. They left a few months later, and I understand they're thriving.

God used me to speak to our assistant pastor a short time later. The word God spoke to her through me confirmed what was in her heart. She'd felt the need to move on and left within a few months. This upset our pastor, who made it obvious he didn't want me there. Right before my first surgery, he and his wife walked to our trailer to speak to me when Carrie wasn't home. He accused me of lying about my feet and asked me why I was mooching off my sister who worked so hard. He ordered me to stay out of his church, and said if he had his way he'd have me run out of town. His wife agreed and added a few unkind words to the slander.

I tried to tell them the truth and explain things, but they didn't want to hear a word I had to say. I walked to the kitchen, lit up a cigarette, took a few puffs, and asked them to go. When they realized I wasn't reacting to their further accusations, they finally left.

I had the first surgery a few weeks later, and the second five weeks after that. The pain was more severe than I thought it would be, and I dreaded every time I had to go to the bathroom, but I had to get up and walk. I thought of the story of the man who complained that he had no shoes. God reminded him of the man who wished he had two feet.

After several months of painful recovery, I could walk with a cane and got my first computer job at a call center. I thought it would be enough to learn computer basics at the library, but, oh, how I had to pray to make it through every day. Here I was, barely computer literate, entering data for insurance claims. Thank God, those days are over. His grace truly is sufficient. It's what got me through.

The next step in my *spiritual* recovery came when I was leaving the credit union one Friday. A gentleman in the elevator complimented my cross, the same one my angel had liked. Our conversation continued in the parking lot, where he invited me to his church. The very next Sunday, my heart found its home at Judah Christian Community Church in Columbus, Ohio.

Being planted in a church is one of the most important things you can do for yourself. Life started when I joined my church. My wonderful pastor, like a spiritual father, taught me how to live with integrity and righteousness. I felt the love and acceptance I've always searched for. Who would have believed that I'd become an ordained evangelist in 2009? But you see, God specializes in people like me. He hung out with the outcasts, the drunks, and the prostitutes. If you let Him, he'll take your mess and make it your message.

God promises beauty for ashes and joy instead of mourning. You only have to repent of your sins and ask Him into your heart, and He'll help you. He'll give you more than you could ask, think, or pray. I promise. He promises. With God, *all* things are possible.

Chapter 12

The God of Second Chances

"Weave in faith and God will find the thread."
Author Unknown

I visited Judah Christian Church five times before I joined; I don't know why it took me so long. I loved the pastor, the music, the worship, the people . . . it was beautiful. It was diverse, nondenominational, multicultural, and multiracial—a "come-as-you-are" church. I seldom missed a service, starving for every word the pastor preached. They fed my spirit and encouraged my soul.

As hope rose in me, I wanted to do something more for God. The gentleman who invited me to church, Pastor Donald Miller, and his brother had founded a street ministry called *Brother to Brother*, with outreaches to prisons, shelters, and nursing homes. Before I could join, I had to meet certain qualifications, including not smoking. I'd tried to quit in the past, but had failed, so immediately asked for prayer.

During a cigarette break at work, someone asked me for a light. I started to offer my half-empty lighter, but God told me to give my new one because I wouldn't need it by the upcoming Friday. On Friday, I invited several friends from work to a special night at church, anticipating with great faith what God would do.

The service was called a "shut-in," which started at nine and lasted until God said it was over. Ours lasted about five hours. We prayed, sang, worshiped, and waited on God. It was February 21, 2003, the night of my miracle. At the start of the second song, God moved me to lay my cigarettes and lighter on the altar. I never looked back. He delivered me on the spot; no more cigarettes, no more cravings.

I had joined *Brother to Brother*, learning all I could from Elder Miller, a wonderful mentor. We visited shelters and youth prisons. About six months after joining the church, I started a ministry called *2ⁿᵈ Chance*. I went to the homeless camps in the woods, under bridges, anywhere I could find them. I'd take food, clothing, and speak about Jesus.

I made some good friends out there. These were good people who had fallen by the wayside. They'd become alcoholics and addicts because they couldn't handle life's challenges the way others could. They had great hearts and wanted to do better, but needed help finding their way out of the holes they'd dug for themselves.

I saw myself in them, settling for what life gives, believing you don't deserve better; no longer living, just surviving; beaten down till nothing matters because you don't matter. By the grace of God, I had family to help me; most of them didn't. Quitting was never an option for me; they'd given up. God had rescued me, and I was going to do my best, with His help, to give them a second chance—one soul at a time.

In the beginning, it was hard to enter their world. I had to prepare for some sorrowful things. Along with pregnant girls, I met a young woman dying of cancer who had completely given up on life and refused our help. She weighed about eighty-five pounds and slept on a concrete slab. I met several war veterans who felt betrayed and forgotten. There were abuse victims as young as eight and as old as seventy. I loved them all. To me there were no lost causes, only lost people.

One Sunday, God told my pastor that some of us would go back to school, no matter what age or circumstance. I knew he meant me, and, within a few months, I began medical assisting school, graduating almost a year later in 2004.

I got a great job for a wonderful Russian doctor at an internal medicine office near my home. She was kind and generous, and took great care of me with bonuses and Christmas presents. I loved my patients like family. They were always giving me little gifts and cards.

When I traveled to Ukraine on a missions trip with my church, it was such an eye opener. We ministered to gypsies there and in Prague and the Czech Republic. Most of the people were poor and had very little, but were rich in spirit. They loved God and were humble and thankful. I taught Sunday school in an orchard, where children sat on the ground while little goats ran in between them. It was so inspiring to see how hungry they were to learn about God. We were able to lead several hundred to Christ; many were children from a local orphanage. I left there thankful for what I had at home and vowed to stop complaining from then on.

Once back at work, I was accused of giving wrong sample to a patient. The doctor believed whoever it was who lied about me. I quit that job, though God vindicated me not long after. I found work as a waitress (my usual fall back), then tried office work but didn't like that either. Other than on-and-off catering, I was unemployed for about two years and having a really rough time. I mowed yards, sold my books at a half-price store, and took whatever odd job I could. I'd pray about gas and bill money, and God always came through. I'd learned how to survive.

My ministry (*2ⁿᵈ Chance*) was growing. We fed more and more of the homeless and joined a homeless coalition. When I heard about human trafficking, I called the City Attorney's office and was referred to a woman who ran a home for victims of this modern-day form of slavery. Before you knew it, we were out on the streets looking for at-risk targets.

I joined a human trafficking coalition and was trained as a speaker and advocate for these victims. I became a passionate abolitionist and was hungry to do more. After all, I'd been a victim of human trafficking without realizing it. One day, I heard God's still, small voice telling me to go to college. Uncertain of how I would pay for it, I took a step of faith and enrolled at Columbus State Community College. Incredible!

Excited but scared, I became a first-generation college student at fifty-seven. I did much better than I could have imagined, achieving a 4.0 GPA more than once and an overall average of 3.8 throughout college. Amazingly, I was actually smart. I won so many scholarships that I exceeded my limit; some were taken back and some applied to my school loan debt. I paid off more bills as an unemployed full-time student than when I worked full time at the doctor's office. That's how God works: more than you could ask, think, or pray.

In 2010, I was named Outstanding Student Leader along with seven others. It was such an honor. I made the Dean's list every quarter and graduated magna cum laude. I'll never forget walking for my diploma, especially since I didn't graduate high school. I'll also never forget what God said to me about six months after I started school: *Going to college is not about graduating and getting a good job until retirement. It's about My healing.* As always, He was exactly right.

I learned about addiction and addictive thought processes, dysfunctional patterns and negative behaviors, setting boundaries and adding new coping skills, and that I wasn't crazy after all. With the knowledge and understanding of how I thought and why, I gained the wisdom to maintain right behavior and help others do the same. You know, you can't help someone else if you're not healthy first. We shouldn't be wounded healers.

During my graduation ceremony, I was one of five people honored. They shared my personal testimony and asked me to stand as the audience applauded. Imagine that! When the Dean handed me my diploma, he said he was very proud of me. He said I was his hero. God knew exactly what I needed. I'd completed something good, my self-esteem never higher.

God knows what's in us; He knows us better than we know ourselves. God has great plans for us, if we'll just trust and believe Him. He's proved it to me, and He'll do it for you.

Chapter 13

More Than I Could Ask, Think, or Pray

"Life is God's novel. Let him write it."
Isaac Bashevis Singer

In conversation one day, Pastor Miller realized that a pastor he'd been talking to needed to meet our pastor because they shared the same vision. Within a matter of weeks, these two pastors met and immediately felt a divine connection and purpose. After much prayer and preparation, they decided to merge churches. This new church was all white, except for an assistant pastor from Africa. Our church was all African-American, except for me and another member I nicknamed Flash, because he loved taking pictures. Something awesome had started, and it was God's doing. We went through several transitions, as God changed and united us. I'm happy to say, our church became stronger than ever.

When God told me to stop doing the homeless ministry, my heart couldn't quit. Because of my initial disobedience, I went through a lot of needless anxiety and frustration. God was taking me into a new season, opening a whole new door.

During college, I'd interned with several social service agencies, including the Salvation Army. I had been a member of the human trafficking coalition, Central Ohio Rescue and Restore (CORRC) since 2007, so it felt like home to work with the ladies I'd gotten to know who had a heart for the same cause. I helped to design a street outreach for prostitutes (trafficked victims) for the Salvation Army that is still going strong today. It was through CORRC that I was introduced to a special court docket for prostitutes, a two-year pilot program in Franklin County Municipal Court for trafficked victims who wanted to start over. They partner with a drug and alcohol rehabilitation program for women, and together they rebuild lives. The program offers real help, with group therapy, one-on-one counseling, and trauma processing.

Ironically, I'd never considered personal counseling. As usual, God made a way. A friend at church had just graduated college for Christian counseling. Without my asking, she offered to see me, and it was free. We did Eye Movement Desensitization Reprocessing (EMDR). During therapy, you recall specific incidents of trauma and, at the same time, the counselor uses a predetermined tapping method on your palms, upper knee, etc. This simultaneous touching/talking brings both sides of the brain into balance. Afterwards you are able to recall the event, but not feel the trauma. It was totally freeing. I'd done research on EDMR while in college and had dreamed of getting therapy. God really does give us our heart's desires!

Within a few months of volunteering at the court program, God laid it on my heart to do makeovers of the girls' apartments. He reminded me what it was like to have nothing and helped me realize how grateful I'd have been to have had this done for me. To help the girls see the contrast between what the world offers and what God could do, I was to wait a few weeks after they moved in to get started. I asked my cousin Donna to help, and we collected whatever we could find at garage sales and thrift stores.

It was humbling to ask a grown woman what design or colors she'd like for her kitchen or bath, when she'd respond, "No one ever asked me that before," or "You mean I have a choice?" I've been in that spot myself, to a lesser degree even today, without money to fix up my place.

When makeover day came, the look on the girls' faces was priceless. They truly appreciated every little detail and knew it was all from God, because as we decorated and rearranged, Donna and I would continually praise Him for it all. I've always shared my faith with the girls. They know God saved my life.

In July 2012, my dear friend Linda and I were discussing fundraising for the makeovers. She wondered if she might ask one of her Sunday school classes for forty or fifty dollars. I suggested asking them to fill a jar with their spare change every week. That's how *Change 4 Change* was born. Our vision was to place jars in churches, businesses, and anywhere that would allow us to raise money to fund the makeovers. I believed for God's favor to have thousands of jars in thousands of places.

We'd been doing makeovers for over two years. I had hoped to continue with the program, but due to unforeseen and unsubstantiated circumstances, I left the program in August 2012. (Guilty until proven innocent, again, but God is still my vindicator.) For the glory of God, however, I do still continue makeovers with other victims in need.

Back in January 2012, I was asked to speak at the Statehouse in Columbus on National Human Trafficking Day. It was a great honor, especially to receive a commendation from House Representative Teresa Fedor.

Afterwards, I had lunch with another trafficked survivor, Theresa Flores, who was a great encouragement to me. We met a few weeks later to discuss a position as her paid assistant with a project God had given her called *Save Our Adolescents from Prostitution* (SOAP). It's an event-driven campaign aimed at distributing thousands of bars of soap with the National Human Trafficking Hotline number to local motels free. Volunteers learn "human trafficking 101" from Theresa, then label the soaps, and place them in motels. Theresa had the Super Bowl in Indianapolis coming up and needed help raising awareness. I gladly accepted. It was a double blessing; I wanted to do more for the victims, and I got paid to do it. SOAP is a very successful outreach, and Theresa continues to be an outstanding inspiration and success story herself.

After speaking at the Ohio Statehouse in January, I received tremendous response to my testimony. I was blessed with several invitations to speak at various events around the state. In May 2012, I spoke at a National Church Conference with Representative Fedor and

Doctor Celia Williamson, a major advocate against human trafficking, along with other noteworthy speakers.

A few weeks later Representative Fedor invited me to testify before the Senate Judiciary Subcommittee on human trafficking and House Bill 262. Called the Safe Harbor Law, this bill provides greater resources and recompense for trafficked victims and stronger penalties and sentences for the trafficker. Bill 262 is going through various legislative stages and should be put into effect soon.

Then Doctor Williamson invited me to speak at her annual anti-human trafficking conference at the University of Toledo in September 2012. It was an awesome experience. I received great feedback from my presentation.

Another senator wanted to help me start a consulting business for law enforcement and other professionals to better deal with victims. She was very gracious and supportive.

We spoke a short time later. She'd been unable to do some of the things she wanted to do because of her busy schedule. I was disappointed with the way things turned out, but not for long. I'd learned a long time ago that if it's supposed to be, it will be and thanked her for her help. It was wonderful to see God use someone so important for somebody like me. Only He could take someone from the crack house to the Statehouse, from living with dealers to dining with senators. What a mighty God we serve!

I trust God completely with my future. He's proven over and over again in every situation that He has my best interest at heart. He opens the right doors at the right time and closes them, too. I realized that I'd put too much hope in what the senator could do, although she had great intentions. I know God can do anything, so I'll keep waiting on Him until He opens the way again.

Encouraged countless times to write my life story, I never thought it was that big a deal. After all, what did I have to offer, a road paved with mistakes? But it's also about the power of God. What have we got to lose? How will we ever walk on water unless we get out of the boat? I'm eternally grateful for where God has brought me and where He's taking me. I may not know what the future holds, but I know Who holds the future.

Chapter 14

Never Despise Small Beginnings

"There are two lasting bequests we can give our children.
One is roots. The other is wings."
Hodding Carter, Jr.

We don't get to pick our parents, but God does, and He doesn't make mistakes. I believe someday my sons and I will have a close and loving relationship again, because God promises to restore all the devil has stolen and give us double for our trouble. Until then, I'll keep the faith and continue praying. I've put them in God's hands, and there's no better place to be.

I'm not making excuses for the kind of mother I was. My sons have paid dearly for my wrong choices. It was never anything they did; they were good boys. I would do anything to change the past. I just want others to see how much damage is caused if you keep pain in your heart or let fear or rejection rule. Take it from someone who knows, sadness and regret can ruin your life. We can't change the past, but we can change the future.

I thank God for my wonderful sons, daughters-in-law, granddaughters, and the rest of my family. I believe He's working it all out. He promises in Romans 8:28 that all things work together for good for those who love the Lord. I'm sure of this: it's never too late and you're never too far gone.

The enemy tries to tell us we're unworthy, but the Bible tells us that Jesus hung out with the drunks and beggars, the prostitutes and outcasts. You can always start over, but the only true way is with God. Jesus said, *"I am the way, the truth, and the life. No one goes to the Father except through Me."* (John 14:6) With Him, all things are possible. God is love, and love never fails. We're all born with a God-shaped hole that only He can fill. We're all in bondage to something, but He died to set the captives free.

I'm a Luke 7:47 woman. It says, *"Though her sins were many she was forgiven much, therefore she loved much."* God has taught me how to let my mess become my message. He's given me wings to fly and leave all the regrets behind. My pain is now my power. It is the purpose and passion of my life, as much as I can, to help others avoid the mistakes I've made.

I believed all my life that I was unworthy, unlovable, didn't deserve goodness or happiness, and got what was coming to me. The devil will always lie to people the world considers outcasts of society. He knows the power and purpose that God has put in us, and he doesn't want us going to heaven or taking anyone with us. I've read the end of the (Bible) story, and the devil is the real loser.

I hope somehow my story touches your life and softens your heart. I hope it opens your eyes to see the truth as it did mine. The very first Scripture I ever read was right after I was saved. James 16:20 says, *"I will turn your sorrow into joy."* God truly did that and continues to do so as long as I give Him all my burdens and worries.

James 4:2 says, *"You have not because you ask not."* God is waiting for you to ask Him for help. If He did it for me, He can do it for you. Just believe. You have nothing to lose. Tomorrow is promised to no man. Don't waste your life in misery and unhappiness. Reach out for all God has for you. He'll never let you down. He'll never give up on you. Our Redeemer lives!

I plan to continue doing makeovers and helping anyone in need. I envision *Change 4 Change* growing more and more. I also believe I'll meet my husband soon. We'll travel nationally and internationally, evangelizing and preaching God's Word. I pray to open *2nd Chance* centers, facilities to help the poor, needy, and anyone who wants to start over. I hope to continue speaking on behalf of trafficked victims and to bring hope to anyone who wants to know God more. I want every person I meet to know the love and hope of Jesus that continues to give my life purpose and power every day. I want to see millions saved, delivered, and set free for the glory of God. I will take as many souls to heaven with me as I can.

There's no sweeter victory than freedom; that's what salvation brings. God's Word says in John 8:36, "*Whom the Son sets free is free indeed!*" That freedom is for you. I pray God's love gives you roots and helps you find your wings. I leave you with Jeremiah 29:11: "*I know the plans I have for you, says the Lord. Plans for good not evil, for a future and a hope.*"

Epilogue

Yes, I'm a hillbilly and proud of it. I'm an original coalminer's daughter, and I'll always cherish my earliest childhood memories. What happened after that has been redeemed.

Looking back, I know my mother did her best for us with what she had. I love her, and I'm very thankful she's my mother. She's a great supporter and encourager in my life. I pray she'll soon get to enjoy her life again.

I carried unforgiveness for a long time, but God helped me see that it kept me a prisoner most of my life. I forgave everyone who ever hurt me, and I hope you will, too. Mothers aren't perfect. We don't come with an instruction manual. We want the best for our children, but sometimes we're so stuck in our own pain that we can't see the way out. I wish I could have made great memories with my two sons, but, as I learned later in life, you can't give away something you don't have.

I could live in regret the rest of my days, but that would only continue the cycle, and I want to have a great life with my granddaughters. Regret kept me a prisoner to my past, and I almost died because of it. I believe I lived to tell my story so that others might see themselves in it. If everything I went through was to keep my sons from repeating my mistakes and experiencing my suffering, then I'd do it all again. They are wonderful fathers and husbands today thanks to our loving and merciful God.

And if my story has touched anyone out there who's just about given up, who feels hopeless and helpless, just remember, you can take God's hand, too. He's waiting for you.

In John 14:6 Jesus said "I am the way, the truth, and the life. No one can come to the father except through me.

If you'd like to make Jesus your personal savior, just pray this prayer out loud to Him right now: Jesus, I repent of all my sins, come into my heart and make me new. I accept you as my savior. Help me to live for you always. In Jesus name, Amen. Halleleujah!